Flashcards

50 Flashcards $7.95

GEORGIA

High School Graduation Test

ENGLISH LANGUAGE ARTS

Preparing Students for the Georgia Performance...

©2006 Hollandays Publishing Corporation

Printed in USA. Minimal p...

Correct each sentence.

1. Under the bed Tiffany was happy to find her notebook.

2. The car with the new wheels speed down the road.

3. Last week Jason found a dog in his best jacket.

4. Although the snow is deep, the children with the new sled slides rapidly downhill.

1

1. Tiffany was happy to find her notebook under the bed.

2. The car with the new wheels speeds down the road.

3. Jason was in his best jacket last week when he found a dog.

4. Although the snow is deep, the children with the new sled slide rapidly downhill.

Define **propaganda** and describe its purpose.

Propaganda – Information that is spread to support a cause

Purpose of Propaganda – To create an emotional connection between the message and the reader or listener

Which sentence is correct? What must be corrected in each of the other three sentences?

1. We were going to the movies, but mom said that we had to wait.

2. Dad needed the car to run an errand, and he don't know when he will be back.

3. Leanna and me played cards for a few minutes.

4. We left for the movies as soon as Dad returned, and we were there in time for the previews.

3

Sentence 4 is correct.

Sentence 1 has a capitalization error (Mom).

Sentence 2 has an error in subject-verb agreement (he doesn't or didn't).

Sentence 3 has a pronoun error (Leanna and I).

1. What is **revision?**

2. List revision strategies.

1. **Revision** - altering and improving the organization and content of an essay

2. **Revision strategies**
   - organize during prewriting to avoid major revisions
   - change or delete sentences that are off topic
   - improve word choice

Choose the correct verb in the parentheses:

1. Many (**arrives, arrive**) early at school each day.

2. The confusion among his students (**is, are**) understandable.

3. Neither of the girls (**wants, want**) to visit the art museum today.

4. It (**don't, doesn't**) matter to me if you eat all of the pizza.

1. Many **arrive** early at school each day.

2. The confusion among his students **is** understandable.

3. Neither of the girls **wants** to visit the art museum today.

4. It **doesn't** matter to me if you eat all of the pizza.

Rewrite the following sentences so that they are correct.

1. "I wish the dogs would stop barking long enough for me to get a little bit of sleep" Moaned my tired mother

2. "Vanessa" her best friend pleaded "Are you still angry at me for the trick I played on you"

3. I wish the cafeteria at kashwee high school served chinese food once in awhile.

4. my english class just finished reading the poem entitled the raven by edgar allan poe and the novel to kill a mockingbird by harper lee.

1. "I wish the dogs would stop barking long enough for me to get a little bit of sleep," moaned my tired mother.

2. "Vanessa," her best friend pleaded, "are you still angry at me for the trick I played on you?"

3. I wish the cafeteria at Kashwee High School served Chinese food once in awhile.

4. My English class just finished reading the poem entitled "The Raven" by Edgar Allan Poe and the novel *To Kill a Mockingbird* by Harper Lee.

What are the elements of an effective **introductory sentence?**

What are the elements of an effective **concluding sentence?**

An effective **introductory sentence** should:

- introduce the main idea
- omit a detailed explanation of any idea
- capture the reader's attention

An effective **concluding sentence** should:

- provide a satisfying ending
- omit new ideas

Define **plot**.

Summarize the plot of a favorite book or film in 6-8 sentences.

Plot - the action of a story

What is **context?**

What is the meaning of **great** in each context?

1. A great crowd gathered outside the stadium.

2. The other writers admired the great book she had written.

3. Thomas Washington was his great-grandfather.

Context is a word's setting. The other words in a sentence create context and determine meaning.

1. large
2. of highest quality or importance
3. one generation removed from the relative named (here, one generation from grandfather)

Steps for success on the English/Language Arts Test

1. For questions that accompany a reading selection - Read the passage, read the question and all answers, and refer to the reading selection to answer questions.

2. For written answers - Use prewriting to plan your answer. Respond to the prompt with organized, detailed writing. Use the editing checklist to improve your answer.

How are choosing the **main idea** and choosing the **best title** for a passage alike and different?

11

Alike - Both require the reader to decide the focus of a passage, to sort through the details and to determine the main idea.

Different - Main ideas are expressed in complete sentences. Titles are expressed in short phrases.

Which underlined section of these sentences requires a change?

The flowers of spring are my favorites.
_____
A

Crocuses daffodils and tulips herald spring and
_____   _____
B   C

affect my mood every year.
_____
D

B - a comma is needed

The flowers of spring are my favorites. Crocuses, daffodils and tulips herald spring and affect my mood every year.

Steps of the Writing Process

- **Prewrite** (brainstorm, organize)
- **Draft**
- **Revise**
- **Edit**
- **Publish** (turn in your essay)

Active Reading Skills

S.U.R.E.

- **Skim** or preview each passage.
- **Underline** key points and focus on the main idea.
- **Reread** if necessary.
- **Engage!** Concentrate on the ideas and visualize characters and setting.

How do writers support
topic sentences and develop
paragraphs?

- Facts
- Examples
- Definitions
- Compare
- Contrast
- Anecdote

Define **style**.

Style is a writer's unique way of telling a story or informing a reader.

Use context clues to define the underlined word:

The <u>disconsolate</u> face of each player told me that this team had lost the game.

17

disconsolate - sad; dejected

Add punctuation and capitalization.

1. she shouted smokey come here

2. the dog a black terrier came dashing toward her

3. good boy she said come inside now smokey

1. She shouted, "Smokey, come here!"

2. The dog, a black terrier, came dashing toward her.

3. "Good boy," she said. "Come inside now, Smokey."

1. What is a **thesis statement?**

2. Describe a good thesis statement.

1. A **thesis statement** states the main idea of an essay.

2. A good thesis statement includes the essay's topic and a specific direction for the paper. It limits the scope of the essay and provides focus for the author and reader.

What is **editing**?

List editing strategies.

Editing - altering and improving the punctuation, spelling, grammar and neatness of an essay

Editing Strategies -
- Read the paper aloud to discover errors.
- Check each sentence for completeness and end punctuation.
- Check legibility of handwriting.

1. What is **point of view?**

2. Describe **first-person point of view** and **third-person point of view.**

1. The perspective from which a story is told is the **point of view.**

2. **First person** - the narrator experiences the story; the narrator uses the word "I"

   Third person - the narrator observes the story
   The third person narrator can be:
   - Omniscient - knows all thoughts and actions of all characters, *or*
   - Limited - knows the thoughts of only one or some characters

Name four steps
for success on the
reading test.

22

1. Read the entire selection.

2. Read the question and all answer choices on each multiple choice question.

3. Refer to the reading selection to answer the question.

4. Write complete answers to the constructed-response questions.

Simile or Metaphor?

1. She was mad as a hornet.

2. Her hair was straw.

3. My love is like a red, red rose.

4. It hasn't rained in a month. My yard is concrete.

1. Simile
2. Metaphor
3. Simile
4. Metaphor

1. What is a **source?**

2. Rank these information sources from most to least reliable:

    A) an article in a gossip magazine

    B) a research study from a major university

    C) an article in a weekly news magazine

    D) information said in a joking manner on a comedy show

3. Is the Internet a reliable source of accurate information?

1. A **source** is the origin of data or information.

2. B, C, A, D

3. Internet users must consider the reliability of each website that they read. The Internet is made up of websites that range from very accurate to totally false. Consider the source of Internet information to determine reliability.

What are the elements of an
effective **concluding paragraph?**

An effective concluding paragraph

- Provides a satisfying end to the essay (summary, call to action or recommendation)

- Introduces no new ideas

What are the elements of an effective introductory paragraph?

An effective introductory paragraph:

- Contains the thesis statement

- Introduces main ideas

- Does not include a detailed explanation of any idea (body paragraphs will contain details)

1. What clues help define a word in context?

2. Use context clues to define each
   word in bold type.

   A) The feeble, **languid** breeze failed
   to move the leaf.

   B) The frowning woman was not **amiable**.

   C) The butterfly flitted rapidly, **eluded** my net
   and flew away.

1. The context is a synonym.

The context is an antonym.

The general meaning of the passage defines the word.

2.

A) The feeble, **languid** breeze failed to move the leaf. **(languid - weak)**

B) The frowning woman was not **amiable**. **(amiable - friendly)**

C) The butterfly flitted rapidly, **eluded** my net and flew away. **(eluded - escaped)**

How can a reader draw a conclusion from text?

What conclusion(s) can you draw from this passage?

The rain poured down. The players and the coach sat in their dugout wondering if this rain would deprive the seniors of their last chance for revenge.

A **conclusion** is a statement that is based on the information in the reading. It is a logical summary based on text.

The baseball team is scheduled to play a team that had beaten them earlier in the season (or the previous year).

Driving on the freeway is easier
than driving in town.

Support this topic sentence in 2 different ways:

1. **with facts**
2. **by contrasting**

Answers will vary but may include:

1. **with facts:** more controlled speed; safely pass slower drivers by changing lanes; everyone going the same way

2. **by contrasting:** no red lights or stop signs on highway; red lights and stop signs to worry about in town; no pedestrians on the highway; have to pay attention to crosswalks in town

Discuss the author's **mood, tone and word choice** in this passage from *The American Crisis* by Thomas Paine.

"These are the times that try men's souls: The summer soldier and the sunshine patriot will in this crisis, shrink from the service of his country; but he that stands it NOW, deserves the love and thanks of man and woman. Tyranny, like hell, is not easily conquered; yet we have this consolation with us, that the harder the conflict, the more glorious the triumph."

Paine's mood is one of passion as he urges his fellow Americans to battle tyranny. Paine's motivating tone calling for action is illustrated by his word choice that includes action verbs, metaphors and words that evoke strong feelings (e.g., love, tyranny, hell, glorious).

Define and give an example.

1. Simile

2. Metaphor

3. Extended Metaphor

1. **Simile** - comparing two things using "as" or "like"
   Example - Her eyes, as blue as the ocean, searched my face with concern.

2. **Metaphor** - comparing two things without using "as" or "like"
   Example - Her ocean-blue eyes searched my face with concern.

3. **Extended Metaphor** - when the metaphor develops beyond one single sentence or phrase. An entire story or poem can be an extended metaphor.
   Example - *Animal Farm* by George Orwell is a book about animals that conveys the author's ideas about political power.

Define **irony** and
give an example.

32

Irony - a literary device in which meaning is contrary to words or actions; there is a mismatch between appearance and reality

Example - "It is as hot as an oven in here!" she said, shivering.

Use context clues to define the underlined word:

We expected a <u>tirade</u>; instead, the teacher praised our effort in a brief, happy speech.

tirade - angry speech

Define **audience**.

34

Audience - the reader or listener

Every author or speaker must tailor his/her delivery to fit the audience.

Use a semicolon to join these sentences in two different ways.

The heat was unbearable.

I went swimming.

35

The heat was unbearable; I went swimming.

The heat was unbearable; therefore, I went swimming.

Correct this sentence in four different ways.

The speakers in that car were very loud, I wanted to get some for my car.

Sample Answers:

The speakers in that car were very loud. I wanted to get some for my car.

The speakers in that car were very loud, and I wanted to get some for my car.

Because the speakers in that car were very loud, I wanted to get some for my car.

The speakers in that car were very loud; therefore, I wanted to get some for my car.

Define **theme.**

List 3 classic themes in literature.

37

Theme is the literary term for the main idea of a piece of writing.

Some classic themes:
coming of age, love, people and nature, people and society, alienation

1. Define **understatement.**

2. Define **hyperbole.**

1. **Understatement** - making something appear smaller or less important than it actually is
Example: "Maybe I should have studied a little more," she said, as her counselor told her she must repeat her sophomore year.

2. **Hyperbole** - obvious exaggeration
Example: I am so tired, I could sleep for a week.

1. Define **setting**.

2. Define **character**. What details can an author use to reveal character?

1. **setting** - the time and place of a story
2. **character** - a person in a story
   - name
   - actions
   - thoughts
   - appearance
   - speech
   - reactions of other characters

1. What is a **source?**

2. Label the following examples as **primary sources** or **secondary sources:**

    A) newspaper editorial that criticizes the governor

    B) report from a research study from a major university

    C) chapter in a textbook

    D) eyewitness testimony

1. A **source** is the origin of data or information.

2. **A** and **C** are secondary sources. **B** and **D** are primary sources.

Define **personification** and give an example.

Personification - giving human qualities or abilities to animals or objects

Example: The clouds wept sadly.

Define and give an example.

1. Allusion

2. Foreshadowing

1. **Allusion** - a reference to literature or an event in history; It is often an indirect reference.
   Example - "If only this school were a bit more like Hogwarts," sighed Jessica.

2. **Foreshadowing** - the use of hints or clues to suggest what may happen later in the story;
   Example - As he entered the dark cave, he sensed that trouble was just around the corner.

"The Passionate Shepherd to His Love"
by Christopher Marlowe

Come live with me and be my love,
And we will all the pleasures prove
That valleys, groves, hills, and fields,
Woods, or steepy mountain yields.

And we will sit upon the rocks,
Seeing the shepherds feed their flocks,
By shallow rivers to whose falls
Melodious birds sing madrigals.

1. What is the **form** of this poem?
2. What is the **rhyme scheme** of the stanzas?

1. The poem is written in lyrical form to describe personal feelings, impressions and thoughts.

2. aabb ccdd

Maple Trees and the Value of American Homes
Source: Maple Tree Growers Association of North America

Homes with a maple tree	$125,000.00
Homes without a maple tree	$74,000.00

1. Why should the source of this information cause readers to be cautious when reading this table?

2. Is it logical to assume that a maple tree adds a great deal of value to a house? What other factors might have affected the value of these homes?

1. The maple tree growers probably have some data to back up these statistics. But they are also trying to sell maple trees, so it is fair for readers to be on the lookout for biased data when reading such a table.

2. No, it is not logical to assume that a maple tree in the yard is enough to increase the value of a home by $51,000. There must be other factors involved, such as, location, house size or quality of construction.

This table and the Maple Tree Growers Association of North America are fictional. But biased data like this is in the news media every day. Read and listen carefully, and consider the sources of information.

Define **symbol**.

45

Symbol - a person or object that stands for something else

Example: As I looked at my old skateboard, I sighed and went to work. (The skateboard represents youth and freedom.)

Specific words convey messages accurately.
Give a more specific word for each word below.

- **Car**
- **Furniture**
- **Teacher**

Explain why an author would choose to use
words that are specific.

Sample answers:

- car - **Corvette**
- furniture - **roll-top desk**
- teacher - **Mr. Rowlands, my chemistry teacher**

Using specific words helps the author establish a clearer, more intriguing scene and message.

Define and give an example.

- **Internal Rhyme**
- **End Rhyme**
- **Slant Rhyme**

- **Internal Rhyme** - poetic device in which a word in the middle of a line rhymes with a word at the end of the same line
Example - Move your feet, lose your seat.

- **End Rhyme** - rhyme in which the last word of each line is the word that rhymes
Example - I hate shopping at the local store. Going there is such a chore.

- **Slant Rhyme** - rhymes created out of words with similar but not identical sounds
Example - I'm going to park my car in that red barn.

Define **paradox**
and give an example.

48

Paradox - a literary term for a seemingly contradictory statement that may nonetheless be true

Example: James Bond is a very well known secret agent.

Define and give an example.

- Alliteration
- Assonance
- Consonance

49

Alliteration - Repetition of the initial letter (generally a consonant) or first sound of several words
Example - Many describe Michelle as a motor mouth.

Assonance - Repetition of vowel sounds, not necessarily at the beginning of words
Example - Will billed Jim for the big crib he built for his kid.

Consonance - Repetition of consonants or consonant sounds, not necessarily at the beginning of words
Example - "Ding-dong," the carolers rang the doorbell, and, as I swung my front door open, they began to sing.

Match the author with his or her period of American literature.

A) Realism

B) Colonial Literature

C) Transcendentalism

D) Romanticism

1) Anne Bradstreet

2) Washington Irving

3) Mark Twain

4) Ralph Waldo Emerson

A) **3** - Mark Twain

B) **1** - Anne Bradstreet

C) **4** - Ralph Waldo Emerson

D) **2** - Washington Irving

Dear Parents,

Here's how to use these flashcards to help your child prepare for

Georgia Language Arts:

- Use the flashcards regularly. Practice 15-30 minutes each night for several weeks before the test.

- Make a check mark on a flashcard each time your child answers that card correctly. After several sessions look for flashcards with no (or few) check marks. Discuss these with your child and seek help from the teacher for these skills.

- Review your child's English class assignments. Discuss repeated errors and focus on improving those skills.

- Read the advice to students on the reverse side of this card and urge your child to follow it.

US $7.95

ISBN 0-9769459-0-8

9 780976 945901

Dear Student,
Here are some ideas to help
you as you prepare for
Georgia Language Arts:

- **Read test selections carefully.** Don't just skim.
Read carefully to understand the main idea and
draw accurate conclusions.

- **Use the text to support answers.** Revisit the text
after you read to find facts.

- **Review rules for sentence construction,
grammar, punctuation, capitalization and
spelling.**

- **Review grammar skills, specific forms of poetry
and examples of figurative speech.**

- **Read questions carefully.** Does the question ask
you to choose the correct answer or the answer
that is NOT correct?

- **Come to the test rested and ready.**

**Remember to study your Flashcards for
15-30 minutes every day for a few weeks
before the test.**

©2006
Hollandays
Publishing
Corporation